"Good morning, this is GOD!"

Teachings, Quotes,
Personal Insights, and Humor
from One of Today's Leading Ministers

by
Joyce Meyer

Harrison House
Tulsa, Oklahoma

"Good morning, this is GOD!" Gift Book —
Teachings, Quotes, Personal Insights, and Humor from One of Today's Leading Ministers
ISBN 1-57794-400-3
(Formerly *Life In The Word — Teachings, Quotes, Personal Insights, and Humor From One of Today's Leading Ministers* ISBN 1-57794-004-0)
Copyright © 2001 by Joyce Meyer
Life In The Word, Inc.
P. O. Box 655
Fenton, Missouri 63026

Published by Harrison House, Inc.
P. O. Box 35035
Tulsa, Oklahoma 74153

Contents

Introduction

This mini-devotional by Joyce Meyer of quotes, teachings, stories and interesting facts about her life and ministry provides practical insights from the wide variety of subjects on which she ministers. Presented in her characteristic straightforward, humorous style, the principles Joyce Meyer capsulizes in this little book, principles which have changed the lives of thousands of people, are easy to reference and daily apply to live victoriously in Jesus!

Begin your day with one of these mini-devotions and give your concerns to God. Then walk through the day enriched with the peace that comes from the deeper knowledge of Him.

Joy and Laughter

There is nothing as tragic as being alive and not enjoying life.

I came that they may have and enjoy life, and have it in abundance (to the full, till it overflows).

John 10:10

7

You have a blood-bought right to enjoy your life.

For ye are bought with a price: therefore glorify God in your body, and in your spirit, which are God's.

1 Corinthians 6:20 KJV

8

Go ahead and enjoy your life while God works on your problems.

He will not allow your foot to slip or to be moved; He Who keeps you will not slumber.

Psalm 121:3

9

Have and Enjoy Life

In John 10:10 we see that Jesus came so we might have and enjoy life. They are two different things to me. It is possible to be alive and not enjoy life.

Webster used the word "relish" to define enjoyment. Think about it like this: People put relish on hot dogs or sandwiches to make them taste better. These foods can be eaten without

the relish, but the relish adds to the flavor, the enjoyment, of them. Life is the same way. We can blandly live our lives, going through the motions of working, accomplishing, doing — and never truly enjoy life.

Enjoying life is a decision, just like putting relish on a hot dog is a decision. Jesus gave us life so we can derive pleasure from being alive, not just so we can go through the motions and try to survive until He comes back for us or takes us home.

Life should be celebrated!

To live as God intends for us to live, the first thing we must do is truly believe that it is God's will for us to experience continual joy.

You will show me the path of life; in Your presence is fullness of joy, at Your right hand there are pleasures forevermore.

Psalm 16:11

12

The reason we can laugh and enjoy life in spite of our current situation or circumstances is because Jesus is our joy.

When Christ, Who is our life, appears, then you also will appear with Him in [the splendor of His] glory.

⤴

Colossians 3:4

The Stages of Life

In some aspects, spiritual growth can be compared to physical growth. I think it would be safe to say that many people do not enjoy their children while they are raising them. At each stage of growth, the parents wish the child was in another stage. If the child is crawling, they wish he were walking, out of

diapers, in school, graduating, getting married, giving them grandchildren, and on and on.

We should learn to enjoy each stage of life as it comes because each has joys and trials uniquely its own. As Christians, we are growing throughout our lifetime. We never stop progressing. Make a decision right now to begin to enjoy yourself while you are striving to reach each new level of victory.

Learn to enjoy each stage of life.

Did You Know?

*A*re you under-laughed? I heard that we need to laugh at least fifteen times a day, three of which need to be hard belly laughs to be at optimum. I can tell you for sure that I was under-laughed, but I am learning. Remember, *a merry heart doeth good like a medicine* . . . (Proverbs 17:22 KJV).

Take your medicine — laugh a little more.

16

Laughter not only makes the journey endurable and even enjoyable; it also helps keep us healthy.

A happy heart is good medicine and a cheerful mind works healing....

Proverbs 17:22

17

Did You Know?

Children laugh easily and freely. As a matter of fact, sometimes, when you watch children play, it seems they giggle almost continually, and over practically nothing. I am sure that they need to grow up some, and that they will as the years go by, but we adults also need some of what they have and display so freely.

Be like a child: learn to laugh more.

*Did You
Know?*

When we come home from our ministry trips, I love to just be at home — in my house. I prefer to eat at home when possible, and I like to watch good, clean family movies on the VCR or television when available. I like to sit around, or walk around with a cup of tea or coffee and look out the windows. I just like to be there.

But, I have noticed that after about three days maximum I start getting bored with what I was loving three days before. There is nothing wrong with me. It is just my God-given nature letting me know that it is time for something different.

We were created for variety.

Created for Variety

Behold, I am doing a new thing! Now it springs forth; do you not perceive and know it and will you not give heed to it? . . . (Isaiah 43:19).

Do you ever get just plain bored — just really tired of doing the same old thing all the time? You want to do something different but you either don't know what to do, or you are

afraid to do the new thing you are thinking about doing? The reason may be because you were created for variety.

I believe God has put creativity in all of us. He is certainly creative and believes in variety. Think of all the varieties of birds, flowers, trees, grass, etc., He has created. People come in a never-ending variety of sizes, shapes and colors, with different personalities.

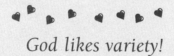

God likes variety!

Did You Know?

My heavenly Father has restored my lost inner child. In other words, now I can trust, love, forgive, live with simplicity in my approach to life; and I am free to enjoy what I do. I no longer have to justify fun. I know it is an important part of life and necessary to maintain right balance. I purposely try to enjoy everything I do. I determine to do so.

To enjoy life to the full, keep it simple.

Relationship and Fellowship

Under the New Covenant, every person's worth and value is based strictly on being "in Christ" by virtue of believing in Him totally as everything that individual needs.

But of him are ye in Christ Jesus, who of God is made unto us wisdom, and righteousness, and sanctification, and redemption.

ॐ

1 Corinthians 1:30 KJV

Once I learned that my value and worth are not in what I do, but in who I am in Christ, I no longer felt that I had to perform for people.

Whatever may be your task, work at it heartily (from the soul), as [something done] for the Lord and not for men.

જીસ

Colossians 3:23

Each one of us is an individual, created by our Father to be different from the person next to us.

I will confess and praise You for You are fearful and wonderful and for the awful wonder of my birth! Wonderful are Your works, and that my inner self knows right well.

Psalm 139:14

Did You Know?

You have a right to be yourself! Do not let the devil steal that right from you!

Are you accepting the fact that you were not created like everyone else, that you are a unique individual? Are you enjoying your uniqueness?

So many people are waging a private war inside themselves, comparing themselves to almost everyone they come near, which causes them to judge themselves or the other person. None of us should be like anyone else. Each of us should be the facet of the Lord that He intends for us to be — uniquely individual — so that corporately we may accomplish God's plan and bring glory to Him.

Make the most of your uniqueness.

26

God will help you be all you can be — all you were originally designed to be. But He will never permit you to be successful at becoming someone else.

For I know the thoughts and plans that I have for you, says the Lord, thoughts and plans for welfare and peace and not for evil, to give you hope in your final outcome.

Jeremiah 29:11

A Personalized Plan

God showed me something powerful. He said, "Every single person is at a different place on the road of life!" Think about it! We all got saved at different times. We have different backgrounds, and some of us have deeper hurts than others. Some people press a little harder than others. Thank God, He has a personalized plan for our lives!

The Lord showed me that, when the trumpet sounds and Jesus comes, Christians will be in many varied places along the road of life. We're not all in the same place now in our outward manifestation of the perfection in Christ, and we won't all be at the same place then. But if each of us has a perfect heart toward God, He sees each one of us as equal. Those who are not quite as perfected as others simply need Jesus a little more. But He's got enough perfection to go around!

Whatever we may need, Jesus is the answer.

Did You Know?

*H*ebrews 7:25 says, **Therefore He is able also to save to the uttermost (completely, perfectly, finally, and for all time and eternity) those who come to God through Him, since He is always living to make petition to God and intercede with Him and intervene for them.**

Wow! What a Scripture! He is able to save me to the uttermost — that means through and through. Jesus is able to save me from whatever is wrong with me! I can't save myself and neither can you! But Jesus can save me, and He can save you!

The solution is Jesus!

30

Did You Know?

*N*o matter how many principles and formulas you and I learn, we will never have any real lasting victory in our Christian life without spending time in personal, private fellowship with the Lord. The victory is not in methods; it is in God.

We are overcomers through
Him Who overcame.

31

Too Busy for God?

A friend of mine had a vision once while she was praying. She saw the Father go into the homes of the people of America, all ready to fellowship and talk to them. He got Himself a chair at the table and sat down. The people got up, and they came, and they went; they came, and they went. They kept telling

God, "Later. Stay right there for just a little while, God. As soon as I get this done, I'm going to talk to You. . . "

The end of the day came, and the girl who saw this said it broke her heart because she saw God, with slumped over shoulders, leave the home. And nobody had ever come to talk to Him that day.

Don't get too busy. If you don't have time to pray and spend time with God, then you are too busy. Take the time to tell God how much you love Him.

God is never too busy for you.

The Lord is ever present and always available to fellowship with us or to help us with our needs.

God is our Refuge and Strength [mighty and impenetrable to temptation], a very present and well-proved help in trouble.

૪ð

Psalm 46:1

34

It is only in the presence of the Lord that we receive the power of the Lord.

... God anointed and consecrated Jesus of Nazareth with the [Holy] Spirit and with strength and ability and power; ... He went about doing good and, in particular, curing all who were harassed and oppressed by [the power of] the devil, for God was with Him.

Acts 10:38

I have discovered the secret of the Spirit-controlled temperament. The key is spending quality personal time with the Lord and receiving help from Him on a regular basis.

. . . those who wait for the Lord [who expect, look for, and hope in Him] shall change and renew their strength and power; they shall lift their wings and mount up [close to God] as eagles [mount up to the sun]; they shall run and not be weary, they shall walk and not faint or become tired.

Isaiah 40:31

36

God's Love and Spirit

If you had been the only person on the face of this earth, He would have gone through all the suffering for you! God loves you with an everlasting love.

For God so loved the world, that he gave his only begotten Son, that whosoever believeth in him should not perish, but have everlasting life.

John 3:16 KJV

Love is not His occupation; it is Who He is. God is always loving us, but often we stop receiving His love, especially if our behavior is not good.

. . . God is love, and he who dwells and continues in love dwells and continues in God, and God dwells and continues in him.

1 John 4:16

38

What people need more than anything else is a revelation of God's love for them personally. I believe this to be the foundation upon which victorious Christian living must stand.

And to know the love of Christ, which passeth knowledge, that ye might be filled with all the fulness of God.

Ephesians 3:19 KJV

39

Knowing that God loves you gives you confidence in Him and trust in His faithfulness.

We love Him, because He first loved us.

ୟୟ

1 John 4:19

40

All blessings will come through letting God love you: greater faith, victory over sin, healing, prosperity and joy.

And He will love you, bless you, and multiply you; He will also bless the fruit of your body and the fruit of your land . . . which He swore to your fathers to give you.

Deuteronomy 7:13

41

If you can believe
that God, Who is
perfect, loves you, then
you can believe that you
are worth loving.

The Lord hath appeared of old unto me, saying, Yea, I have loved thee with an everlasting love: therefore with lovingkindness have I drawn thee.

Jeremiah 31:3 KJV

God graciously revealed to me, through the Holy Spirit, His love for me personally. That single revelation has changed my entire life and my walk with Him.

. . . it is no longer I who live, but Christ (the Messiah) lives in me; and the life I now live in the body I live by faith in (by adherence to and reliance on and complete trust in) the Son of God, Who loved me and gave Himself up for me.

Galatians 2:20

43

Did You Know?

I no longer try to please God to obtain His love. I have freely received His unconditional love, and I desire to please Him because of what He has already done for me.

What I have just written is very important. Look it over again and again. For me, it is the pivotal point between religion and relationship.

Receive God's love and His Spirit.

There have been several things that God has done that have changed my life radically. One of those things was baptizing me in the Holy Spirit.

John answered them all by saying, I baptize you with water; but He Who is mightier than I is coming, the strap of Whose sandals I am not fit to unfasten. He will baptize you with the Holy Spirit and with fire.

Luke 3:16

Did You Know?

The Lord has restored my emotions and my mind. My will has been delivered from rebellion. I no longer need to control. I am led instead of being driven — led by the Holy Spirit instead of driven by fear and insecurity.

Be led by the Spirit.

The only hope of not being deceived these days is to learn to walk by the Spirit — to be led by the Spirit, not by the flesh.

But I say, walk and live [habitually] in the [Holy] Spirit [responsive to and controlled and guided by the Spirit]; then you will certainly not gratify the cravings and desires of the flesh (of human nature without God).

Galatians 5:16

Did You Know?

The church should be bubbling over with life. It should be vibrant, alive, active, energized, peaceful and joy filled. I believe with all my heart, as a result of my own experience — in addition to what I have watched other people go through — that a wrong approach to God will totally prevent this kind of vitalized living.

A legalistic, religious approach steals life. It does not nourish it. Remember, Paul said, "The Law kills, but the Spirit makes alive." When we follow the Spirit, we feel alive. When we follow the Law, it drains the life out of us.

Law is death, but Spirit is life.

Authority and Victory

God desires to restore you and me to our rightful position of authority. We were born destined for the throne, not the ash heap of life.

Let us then fearlessly and confidently and boldly draw near to the throne of grace . . . that we may receive mercy [for our failures] and find grace to help in good time for every need [appropriate help and well-timed help, coming just when we need it].

Hebrews 4:16

49

If we are ever to have real victory, you and I have to learn the simple scriptural truth that we have not because we ask not.

. . . You do not have, because you do not ask.

James 4:2

50

With Jesus inside us, we have the power to do what we could never do on our own.

To whom God was pleased to make known how great for the Gentiles are the riches of the glory of this mystery, which is Christ within and among you, the Hope of [realizing the] glory.

Colossians 1:27

Did You Know?

There is a temptation to run away from our problems, but the Lord says that we are to go through them. The good news is that He has promised that we will never have to go through them alone. He will always be there to help us in every way. He has said to us, "Fear not, for I am with you."

Don't be afraid; use your power.

Use the name of Jesus, the power of attorney that He has given you, one of the major weapons with which you defend yourself and attack the kingdom of darkness.

... at the name of Jesus every knee should bow, of things in heaven, and things in earth, and things under the earth.

Philippians 2:10 KJV

Did You Know?

Early one morning as I got out of bed, immediately worry leaped into my mind — that is the way the devil operates. He likes to attack us at our weakest moment, such as when we first get up and are still groggy, half-awake and incoherent. That illustrates an important principle: Satan never moves against strength; he only moves against weakness.

As my mind began to revolve around and around that thought the devil had placed in my consciousness, the Lord spoke to me and said, "Joyce, live out of your spirit; don't live out of your head." That was such practical counsel that I have never forgotten it.

Resist the devil at his onset.

Come against Satan when he is trying to get a foothold, and he will never get a stronghold.

... be vigilant and cautious at all times, for that enemy of yours, the devil, roams around like a lion roaring [in fierce hunger], seeking someone to seize upon and devour. Withstand him; be firm in faith [against his onset — rooted, established, strong, immovable, and determined]....

1 Peter 5:8,9

The Purpose of Faith

We must remember that the devil is not going to just sit back and allow us to take new ground without putting up a fight. Any time we begin to make progress in building the Kingdom of God, our enemy is going to come against us.

Many times the mistake we make is trying to use faith to get to the place where there is total freedom from trouble. The

purpose of faith is not always to keep us from having trouble; it is often to carry us through trouble. If we never had any trouble, we wouldn't need any faith.

In our own experience, my husband Dave and I live in a tremendous amount of victory because we have learned to stand our ground and back the devil off our property, to drive him out of different areas in our lives. Learning to be stable in hard times is one of the best ways to do this.

Resist the devil, and he will flee.

The devil will give up when he sees that you are not going to give in.

So be subject to God. Resist the devil [stand firm against him], and he will flee from you.

James 4:7

Did You Know?

In Deuteronomy 7:22, Moses told the children of Israel that the Lord would drive out their enemies before them "little by little."

Between each victory in our lives, there is a time of waiting. During this time the Holy Spirit deals with us, opening to us new revelations, helping us to face and receive even greater truths. The waiting is usually difficult for most of us because impatience is always present within us to stir up dissatisfaction. We want everything now!

Patience is as important as power.

59

Victory is not the absence of problems; it is the presence of power.

But thanks be to God, Who gives us the victory [making us conquerors] through our Lord Jesus Christ.

1 Corinthians 15:57

Did You Know?

According to the Scriptures, Satan seeks to build strong-holds in our minds. Strongholds are lies that are believed. A person who believes a lie is deceived. When an individual believes that wrong is right, he has fallen into deception. Satan works through deception, but the knowledge of the Word is the believer's defense and victory.

No person will ever live a truly victorious life without being a sincere student of the Word of Almighty God.

God's Word is truth and power, life and peace.

61

Prayer and Peace

When you are in trouble, go to the Throne before you go to the phone.

Let us then fearlessly and confidently and boldly draw near to the throne of grace . . . that we may receive mercy [for our failures] and find grace to help in good time for every need [appropriate help and well-timed help, coming just when we need it].

Hebrews 4:16

I was frustrated until I learned to quit either trying to do everything on my own or running to others with my problems rather than running to God.

Do not fret or have any anxiety about anything, but in every circumstance and in everything, by prayer and petition (definite requests), with thanksgiving, continue to make your wants known to God.

Philippians 4:6

First of all, the Lord taught me that I had to pray for what He put on my heart, not for what everyone else wanted to put on my heart.

...the [Holy] Spirit comes to our aid and bears us up in our weakness; for we do not know what prayer to offer nor how to offer it worthily as we ought, but the Spirit Himself goes to meet our supplication and pleads in our behalf with unspeakable yearnings and groanings too deep for utterance.

Romans 8:26

Did You Know?

A person who learns to abide in the Word and let the Word abide in him will have power in prayer. When an individual has power in prayer, he has power over the enemy.

People who make the Word of God a small part of their lives will know only partial truth and will experience only limited freedom, but those who abide in it will know the full truth and will experience complete freedom. The same principle works with effective prayer.

Abiding in the Word increases prayer power.

The Holy Spirit works only in an atmosphere of peace. There is power in peace.

For the kingdom of God is not meat and drink; but righteousness, and peace, and joy in the Holy Ghost.

Romans 14:17 KJV

66

The Mind and Controlling One's Thoughts

The mind is the battlefield where our war with Satan is either won or lost.

[Inasmuch as we] refute arguments and theories and reasonings and every proud and lofty thing that sets itself up against the [true] knowledge of God; and we lead every thought and purpose away captive into the obedience of Christ (the Messiah, the Anointed One).

2 Corinthians 10:5

Our thoughts are silent words that only we and the Lord hear, but those words affect our inner man, our health, our joy and our attitude.

Finally, brethren, whatsoever things are true, whatsoever things are honest, whatsoever things are just, whatsoever things are pure, whatsoever things are lovely, whatsoever things are of good report; if there be any virtue, and if there be any praise, think on these things.

Philippians 4:8 KJV

Did You Know?

Thinking about what you're thinking about is very valuable because Satan usually deceives people into thinking that the source of their misery or trouble is something other than what it really is.

He wants them to think they are unhappy due to what is going on around them (their circumstances), but the misery is actually due to what is going on inside them (their thoughts).

Think about what you are thinking about!

No Confusion

I was holding a meeting in Kansas City, and approximately 300 people were in attendance. I felt led to ask how many of them were currently confused over some issue in their life. To my astonishment, I only saw two people who did not raise their hand, and one of them was my husband.

If I saw correctly, that means 298 out of 300 people were confused. That is 99.3 percent. As I began to check with various groups, I found this to be the case almost everywhere.

As I pondered it and asked the Lord to show me what causes confusion, He said, "Tell them to stop trying to figure everything out, and they will stop being confused." Now I realize that is exactly why I am not suffering with confusion anymore. I still have plenty of things in my life that I do not understand, but there is a major difference now. God has delivered me from trying to figure everything out.

God is not the author of confusion.

You can look at a person's attitude and know what kind of thinking is prevalent in his life.

For as he thinks in his heart, so is he...

Proverbs 23:7

72

Did You Know?

Enough can never be said about the power of being positive. God is positive, and if you and I want to flow with Him, we must get on the same wave length and begin to think positively. I am not talking about exercising mind control, but simply about being an all-around, positive person.

Have a positive outlook and attitude. Maintain positive thoughts and expectations. Engage in positive conversation.

Jesus certainly displayed a positive outlook and attitude. He endured many difficulties including personal attacks. Yet in the midst of all these negatives He remained positive. He always had an uplifting comment, an encouraging word; He always gave hope to all those He came near.

Better to be positive and wrong than negative and right.

73

I would rather stay positive and get 50 percent good results, than stay negative and get 100 percent bad results.

From the fruit of his words a man shall be satisfied with good, and the work of a man's hands shall come back to him [as a harvest].

Proverbs 12:14

Practice being positive in each situation that arises. Even if whatever is taking place at the moment is not so good, expect God to bring good out of it.

We are assured and know that [God being a partner in their labor] all things work together and are [fitting into a plan] for good to and for those who love God and are called according to [His] design and purpose.

Romans 8:28

75

Did You Know?

If you want to live the resurrection life that Jesus has provided, then seek that new, powerful life by setting your mind and keeping it set on things above, not on things on the earth.

Many believers want the good life, but they are passively sitting around wishing that something good would happen to them. Often, they are jealous of others who are living in victory and are resentful that their own lives are so difficult.

If you desire victory over your problems, you must have backbone and not just wishbone! You must be active — not passive. Right action begins with right thinking. Don't be passive in your mind. Start today choosing right thoughts.

Develop backbone, not wishbone!

The Word of God and Positive Confession

Nothing will change in your life without knowledge of God's Word.

My people are destroyed for lack of knowledge....

Hosea 4:6

77

*The more time
a person spends
meditating on the Word,
the more he will reap
from the Word.*

... Be careful what you are hearing. The measure [of thought and study] you give [to the truth you hear] will be the measure [of virtue and knowledge] that comes back to you — and more [besides] will be given to you who hear.

Mark 4:24

Words are seeds.
What we speak we
sow, and what we
sow, we reap!

Be not deceived; God is not mocked: for whatsoever a man soweth, that shall he also reap.

Galatians 6:7 KJV

The Name of Jesus Prevailed!

A friend of mine was driving through an intersection one day and his little three- or four-year-old son was in the car with him. The car door flew open, and the little boy rolled out of the vehicle right into the middle of traffic coming from four ways! The last thing my friend saw was a set of car wheels just about on top of his son — moving at a very fast rate of speed. All he knew to do was cry, "JESUS!"

As soon as he could bring his car to a halt, he jumped out and ran to his son, who was perfectly all right. But the man driving the car that had almost hit the child was absolutely hysterical. My friend went over to him and started trying to comfort him.

"Man, don't be upset!" he said. "My son is all right, he's okay. Don't be concerned about it. Just thank God you were able to stop!"

"You don't understand!" the man responded, "I never touched my brakes!"

There is power in the name of Jesus!

The praising life is the powerful life!

And when they began to sing and to praise, the Lord set ambushments against the men of Ammon, Moab, and Mount Seir who had come against Judah, and they were [self-] slaughtered.

2 Chronicles 20:22

Did You Know?

*P*lacing our faith in God's Word honors Him. Jesus is the Mighty Warrior, the Captain of the Host. He is leading His people into victory. I do not believe that we have to live in fear in these last days. No matter how difficult life may seem, God has promised to provide for His own. He has assured us that we can live in victory if we keep our eyes on Him.

Part of keeping our eyes on Him is keeping His ways and walking in His instructions. All through the Bible we are told to exalt the Word, the name and the blood, to put confidence in the power that is invested in them.

We will walk in victory if we do what the Lord says.

*The Word of God is
the twoedged sword
that is your weapon
of offense with which
you are able to
defend yourself.*

For the word of God is quick, and powerful, and sharper than any twoedged sword, piercing even to the dividing asunder of soul and spirit, and of the joints and marrow, and is a discerner of the thoughts and intents of the heart.

Hebrews 4:12 KJV

84

We can complain and remain, or praise and be raised.

Thank [God] in everything [no matter what the circumstances may be, be thankful and give thanks], for this is the will of God for you [who are] in Christ Jesus [the Revealer and Mediator of that will].

1 Thessalonians 5:18

85

When we murmur, gripe, and complain, we are giving a critical appraisal of the God we serve.

Neither let us tempt Christ, as some of them also tempted, and were destroyed of serpents. Neither murmur ye, as some of them also murmured, and were destroyed of the destroyer. Now all these things happened unto them for ensamples: and they are written for our admonition, upon whom the ends of the world are come.

1 Corinthians 10:9-11 KJV

86

Did You Know?

We all have a great tendency to exaggerate horribly when we feel pressured. We magnify things, blowing them all out of proportion and making them sound much worse than what they really are. The careless words we speak in the heat of the moment may not mean much to us, but they definitely carry weight in the spiritual realm.

When we complain, God takes it personally!

Breakthrough

I recommend having a list of confessions — things that can be backed up by the Word of God — which you speak out loud over your life, your family, and your future.

When I first began learning these principles I am sharing with you in this book, I was terribly negative. God began teaching me that I should not think and say negative things. I obeyed, and one result was that I became happier, because a negative person cannot be happy.

After a period of time had elapsed, I felt my circumstances really were not any different. I asked the Lord about it, and He said, "You have stopped talking negative, but you are not saying anything positive." That was my first lesson in "calling those things which be not as if they were." I had not been taught it by anyone else; God was teaching me Himself, and it proved to be one of the major breakthroughs in my life.

Faith and Trust

We do not need self-confidence; we need God-confidence!

It is better to trust in the Lord than to put confidence in man.

Psalm 118:8 KJV

We must remember that the most important thing in receiving God's blessings is not our great faith but His great faithfulness.

Through faith also Sara herself received strength to conceive seed, and was delivered of a child when she was past age, because she judged him faithful who had promised.

Hebrews 11:11 KJV

91

Faith is not the price that buys God's blessing; it is the hand that receives His blessing. The price was paid for us by Jesus Christ on the cross.

Blessed be the God and Father of our Lord Jesus Christ, who hath blessed us with all spiritual blessings in heavenly places in Christ.

Ephesians 1:3 KJV

Faith is of the heart, and you get it only through a relationship of loving fellowship with God.

For the which cause I also suffer these things: nevertheless I am not ashamed: for I know whom I have believed, and am persuaded that he is able to keep that which I have committed unto him against that day.

2 Timothy 1:12 KJV

93

Faith has to be activated if it is to work, and one of the ways we activate it is through our words.

Truly I tell you, whoever says to this mountain, Be lifted up and thrown into the sea! and does not doubt at all in his heart but believes that what he says will take place, it will be done for him.

Mark 11:23

Faith, like muscle, is strengthened by "using" it, not by talking about it.

You see that [his] faith was cooperating with his works, and [his] faith was completed and reached its supreme expression [when he implemented it] by [good] works.

James 2:22

Did You Know?

There was a time in my life when I was convinced that if I said something, it had to happen because I said it. The mistake I made was thinking that it was my faith and my confession that made what I said come to pass. I forgot that in order to receive anything from God I had to put my trust in Him and not in my words or actions.

The Lord had to teach me to keep my eyes on Him and not on a method or formula. I believe in confessing the Word. I teach it and do it daily. God works through it, and my faith remains in Him, not my confession.

Trust God, not your words or actions.

One of the ways we maintain our liberty is through frequent reminders of who we are in Christ.

Let us hold fast the profession of our faith without wavering; (for he is faithful that promised).

&

Hebrews 10:23 KJV

97

Believe what the Word says you are, and that is what you will become. Believe what the devil says you are, and you will become that. The choice is yours.

For as he thinks in his heart, so is he....

Proverbs 23:7

98

One of the tools the Spirit uses to crucify our flesh is unanswered questions. When we do not know the answer, we have to trust God.

And they that are Christ's have crucified the flesh with the affections and lusts.

Galatians 5:24 KJV

99

Did You Know?

In one of the first stages of progress in my ministry, God instructed me to quit my well-paying, full-time job in order to prepare for ministry, which I finally did.

I began by teaching home Bible studies, which went on for about five years. The meeting grew so large that I started teaching two meetings — one in the morning and the second in the evening. Even though Dave and I were experiencing severe financial stress at that time, I received nothing financially for those meetings.

I eventually learned that God did not want me to know where my provision was going to come from. He wanted to establish Himself as my Source.

Not only is He Alpha and Omega,
He is everything in between.

100

God can make miracles out of mistakes!

And Jesus looking upon them, saith, With men it is impossible, but not with God: for with God all things are possible.

Mark 10:27 KJV

101

Doubt and Unbelief

One evening I was walking around my house trying to do some household things, and I was so miserable. I did not have any joy — there was no peace in my heart. I kept asking the Lord, "What's wrong with me?"

About that time the phone rang and, while I was talking, I thumbed through a box of Scripture cards someone had sent

me. I pulled out Romans 15:13, May the God of your hope so fill you with all joy and peace in believing [through the experience of your faith] that by the power of the Holy Spirit you may abound and be overflowing (bubbling over) with hope.

I saw it!

My whole problem was doubt and unbelief. I was making myself unhappy by believing the devil's lies. I was being negative. I could not have joy and peace because I was not believing. It is impossible to have joy and peace and live in unbelief.

Without faith, there is no joy, no peace, no hope.

Did You Know?

I have had to learn and am still learning what simplicity is and how to approach things with a simple attitude. One of the things I have learned is that believing is much simpler than doubting.

Doubt brings in confusion and often depression. It causes us to speak doubtful and negative things out of our mouths.

Believing, on the other hand, releases joy and leaves us free to enjoy life while God is taking care of our circumstances and situations.

Believing is so much simpler than not believing.

104

The attitude of faith brings us into rest.

For we which have believed do enter into rest, as he said, As I have sworn in my wrath, if they shall enter into my rest: although the works were finished from the foundation of the world.

Hebrews 4:3 KJV

God's Grace and Favor

Grace can be defined as God's willingness to use His ability in your life to meet all your needs.

For by grace are ye saved through faith; and that not of yourselves: it is the gift of God: not of works, lest any man should boast.

Ephesians 2:8,9 KJV

106

Did You Know?

Every time you feel frustrated and confused, it is a sign you are out of grace and into works.

When you have a problem in your life that you do not know how to handle, what you need is not more figuring and reasoning, but more grace. If you can't see a solution to your problem, then you need the Lord to reveal it to you.

The more you worry and reason, the more you fret and strain and turn the problem over in your mind, the more unlikely you are to see the solution to it.

Do not frustrate the grace of God.

Grace is an enablement, the favor and power of the Holy Spirit to help you do whatever needs to be done.

And he said unto me, My grace is sufficient for thee: for my strength is made perfect in weakness. Most gladly therefore will I rather glory in my infirmities, that the power of Christ may rest upon me.

2 Corinthians 12:9 KJV

Did You Know?

You and I don't have a problem that is too big for the grace of God. If our problem gets bigger, God's grace gets bigger. If our problem multiplies, so that we go from one to two or three or more, the grace of God also multiplies so that we are able to handle them.

It doesn't take any more faith to believe God for the answer to three problems than for the answer to two problems or even one problem. Either our God is big enough to handle whatever we face, or He's not. What is impossible with man is possible with God. (Luke 18:27.)

Where weakness abounds,
God's grace abounds even more!

109

Grace is not the freedom to sin; it is the power to live a holy life.

For the grace of God that bringeth salvation hath appeared to all men, teaching us that, denying ungodliness and worldly lusts, we should live soberly, righteously, and godly, in this present world.

Titus 2:11, 12 KJV

Did You Know?

Grace is God doing us a favor, coming in with His power and might to accomplish in and through us what we don't deserve for Him to do. And all we can do is to be filled with gratitude and thanksgiving.

In fact, I don't think we can be truly grateful and thankful until we fully understand the grace of God. Once we grasp the fact that every good thing we have comes to us by the goodness of God, what is there left for us but gratitude and thanksgiving?

Thank God for His grace!

God delights in giving His children favor.

For You, Lord, will bless the [uncompromisingly] righteous [him who is upright and in right standing with You]; as with a shield You will surround him with goodwill (pleasure and favor).

Psalm 5:12

112

Did You Know?

God wants to give you favor, just as He gave favor to Joseph, but in order to receive that favor, you must do what Joseph did and believe for it. Joseph maintained a good attitude in a bad situation. He had a "faith attitude," and God gave him favor.

When God's favor is upon you, people like you for no particular reason, and they want to bless you.

To receive favor,
you must show yourself faithful.

113

Supernatural Favor

Almost twenty-five years ago when I first started ministering, I was scared. I was afraid of being rejected.

I knew that there were people, especially new people, who came to my meetings with a judgmental eye. I was overly cautious about everything I said and did because I wanted everyone to like me and accept me.

That is not normal. And it won't work. Trying to get favor on your own is not only hard work; it is often pointless. Usually the harder you try to please everyone, the more mistakes you make and the less people are attracted to you.

When I found out about supernatural favor, I was just working myself to a frazzle trying to win the approval and acceptance of others. From that time on, I began to believe God for His supernatural favor, and it took the pressure off me. No longer did I have to worry about what kind of impression I was making.

True favor comes from God, not man.

You have as much right to God's favor as anyone else. Learn to avail yourself of it and walk in it.

Let not mercy and truth forsake thee: bind them upon thy neck; write them upon the table of thine heart: so shalt thou find favour and good understanding in the sight of God and man.

Proverbs 3:3, 4 KJV

Patience and Obedience

Impatient people often do not hang around long enough to see the finish of really great things because great things take so much time to mature.

For the vision is yet for an appointed time and it hastens to the end [fulfillment]; it will not deceive or disappoint. Though it tarry, wait [earnestly] for it, because it will surely come; it will not be behindhand on its appointed day.

Habakkuk 2:3

Under pressure people improve more rapidly when they remain patient.

And so it was that he [Abraham], having waited long and endured patiently, realized and obtained [in the birth of Isaac as a pledge of what was to come] what God had promised him.

Hebrews 6:15

118

Did You Know?

One thing helped me tremendously to begin to enjoy a peaceful life. I realized it was useless and extremely frustrating to try to do something about something I could not do anything about.

Are you frustrating yourself trying to make things happen? God has a perfect timing for everything. You must wait on His timing.

Take a new attitude toward waiting.

Timing plays an important part in learning to trust God. If He did everything we asked for immediately, we would never grow and develop. Timing and trust are twins.

In order that you may not grow disinterested and become [spiritual] sluggards, but imitators, behaving as do those who through faith (by their leaning of the entire personality on God in Christ in absolute trust and confidence in His power, wisdom, and goodness) and by practice of patient endurance and waiting are [now] inheriting the promises.

ॐ

Hebrews 6:12

Did You Know?

It is impossible to enjoy waiting if you don't know how to wait patiently. Pride prevents patient waiting because the proud person thinks so highly of himself that he believes he should never be inconvenienced in any way.

Although we are not to think badly of ourselves, we are also not to think too highly of ourselves. It is dangerous to lift ourselves up to such an elevated place that it causes us to look down on others. If they are not doing things the way we want, or as quickly as we think they should be done, we behave impatiently.

A humble person will not
display an impatient attitude.

I have discovered that patience is not the ability to wait, but the ability to keep a good attitude while waiting.

Better is the end of a thing than the beginning of it, and the patient in spirit is better than the proud in spirit.

Ecclesiastes 7:8

Believing makes waiting more endurable.

But if we hope for what is still unseen by us, we wait for it with patience and composure.

Romans 8:25

123

The Fruit of Patience

If you remember, an impatient attitude was one of the wilderness mentalities that kept the Israelites wandering in the wilderness for forty years.

How could these people possibly be ready to go into the Promised Land and drive off the current occupants so they

could possess the land if they could not even remain patient and steadfast during a little inconvenience?

I really encourage you to work with the Holy Spirit as He develops the fruit of patience in you. The more you resist Him, the longer the process will take. Learn to respond patiently in all kinds of trials, and you will find yourself living a quality of life that is not just endured but enjoyed to the full.

Impatience breeds frustration;
patience produces peace.

God is not obligated to anoint what He does not initiate.

And I thank Christ Jesus our Lord, who hath enabled me, for that he counted me faithful, putting me into the ministry.

1 Timothy 1:12 KJV

126

If the Holy Spirit says that something is good, then do it, but if He says no — out it should go.

For it has seemed good to the Holy Spirit and to us not to lay upon you any greater burden than these indispensable requirements.

Acts 15:28

Good intentions are not obedience. Action taken based on God's Word is obedience.

But be doers of the Word [obey the message], and not merely listeners to it, betraying yourselves [into deception by reasoning contrary to the Truth].

James 1:22

Humility and Forgiveness

God uses humble men and women, not those who think they are capable in themselves.

Humble yourselves [feeling very insignificant] in the presence of the Lord, and He will exalt you [He will lift you up and make your lives significant].

James 4:10

God chooses the weak and foolish things of this world, on purpose, so that people look at them and say, "It has to be God!"

. . . God selected (deliberately chose) what in the world is foolish to put the wise to shame, and what the world calls weak to put the strong to shame.

1 Corinthians 1:27

When we see what God has done for us through Jesus Christ, and how little we can ever deserve it, it should provoke humility — God's starting place for power.

Likewise, ye younger, submit yourselves unto the elder. Yea, all of you be subject one to another, and be clothed with humility: for God resisteth the proud, and giveth grace to the humble.

1 Peter 5:5 KJV

131

The Advocate

It is interesting to note that Jesus never defended Himself. The Bible says that He entrusted Himself to God in everything. In the midst of being abused, He entrusted everything, including Himself, to the One Who judges fairly (see 1 Peter 2:23). Jesus went about doing God's business — doing good and, in particular, curing all who were oppressed of the devil.

When we entrust ourselves totally to God and get busy doing His work instead of spending all of our time trying to protect ourselves, our self-constructed walls will come down. We need to let our lives convince others that our hearts are in the right place instead of trying to convince them by defending ourselves verbally.

If you have taken up your own defense, I ask you to remember that Jesus is your Advocate. That means He is your lawyer — the One Who will plead your case. Let Him be your defense.

Humility requires discipline of the tongue.

133

Did You Know?

*O*ne time while I was reading about Smith Wigglesworth and his great faith, I was tremendously impressed by all the wonderful things he did, like healing the sick and raising the dead. I thought, "Lord, I know I'm called, but I could never do anything like that."

Suddenly the Lord spoke to me and said, "Why not? Aren't you as big a mess as anybody else?"

You see, we have it backwards. We think God is looking for people who have "got it together." But that is not true. He is looking for those who will humble themselves and allow Him to work His will and way through them.

Aren't you as big a mess as anybody else?

134

Forgiveness is a gift given to those who do not deserve it.

In Him we have redemption (deliverance and salvation) through His blood, the remission (forgiveness) of our offenses (shortcomings and trespasses), in accordance with the riches and the generosity of His gracious favor.

Ephesians 1:7

135

Did You Know?

If you believe that you must be perfect to be worthy of love and acceptance, then you are a candidate for a miserable life because you will never be perfect as long as you are in an earthly body.

You may have a perfect heart, in that your desire is to please God in all things, but your performance will not match your heart's desire until you get to heaven. You can improve all the time and keep pressing toward the mark of perfection, but you will always need Jesus as long as you are here on this earth. There will never come a time when you will not need His forgiveness and His cleansing.

God's answer for imperfection is forgiveness.

Did You Know?

*G*od wants to give us the gift of forgiveness. When we confess our sins to Him, He forgives us of our sins, puts them away from Him as far as the East is from the West, and remembers them no more. But for us to benefit from that forgiveness, we must receive it by faith.

Many years ago when I was first developing my relationship with the Lord, each night I would beg His forgiveness for my past sins. One evening as I knelt beside my bed, I heard the Lord say to me, "I forgave you the first time you asked, but you have not received My gift because you have not forgiven yourself."

Have you received God's gift of forgiveness?

137

It is not possible to have good emotional health while harboring bitterness, resentment and unforgiveness. Unforgiveness is poison!

Be gentle and forbearing with one another and, if one has a difference (a grievance or complaint) against another, readily pardoning each other; even as the Lord has [freely] forgiven you, so must you also [forgive].

Colossians 3:13

We need to bear each other's weaknesses, realize we all have plenty of them and pray for one another.

Bear (endure, carry) one another's burdens and troublesome moral faults, and in this way fulfill and observe perfectly the law of Christ (the Messiah) and complete what is lacking [in your obedience to it].

જી

Galatians 6:2

Make it your business to be friendly and be a blessing to people in the body of Christ.

And become useful and helpful and kind to one another, tender-hearted (compassionate, understanding, loving-hearted), forgiving one another [readily and freely], as God in Christ forgave you.

Ephesians 4:32

Courage and Confidence

It is impossible to be afraid if you have a personal revelation that God loves you.

There is no fear in love; but perfect love casteth out fear: because fear hath torment. He that feareth is not made perfect in love.

໒ঞ

1 John 4:18 KJV

141

Facing the Storms of Life

Jesus did not come to remove all opposition from our lives, but rather to give us a different approach to the storms of life. We are to take His yoke upon us and learn of Him. (See Matthew 11:29). That means that we are to learn His ways, to approach life in the same way He did.

Jesus did not worry, and we do not have to worry either!

If you are waiting to have nothing to worry about before you stop worrying, then you will have to wait a long time, because that time may never come. I am not being negative. I am being honest!

Matthew 6:34 suggests that we not worry about tomorrow because each day will have sufficient trouble of its own. Jesus Himself said that, and He certainly was not negative. Being at peace, enjoying the rest of God in the midst of the storm, gives much glory to the Lord because it proves that His ways work.

*You will always have something
NOT to worry about!*

Just relax and let God be God.

[Earnestly] remember the former things, [which I did] of old; for I am God, and there is no one else; I am God, and there is none like Me.

ஃ

Isaiah 46:9

144

Did You Know?

I believe we work harder to avoid emotional pain than we do physical pain. Therefore, we build many elaborate defense systems to protect our emotions from the pain of rejection. We put up an invisible (but real) wall between us and anyone who might be able to hurt us.

You see, Satan works in many different ways to steal your freedom and your joy. These two go together! If Satan steals your freedom, he will also steal your joy. You will end up living in a little box, always trying to do what you think will be acceptable to everybody else, never being led by the Holy Spirit within you.

Be aware of the devil's devices.

There is only one thing that can be done about the past, and that is forget it.

Brethren, I count not myself to have apprehended: but this one thing I do, forgetting those things which are behind, and reaching forth unto those things which are before, I press toward the mark for the prize of the high calling of God in Christ Jesus.

Philippians 3:13, 14 KJV

Whenever the devil reminds you of your past, remind him of his future.

... But woe to you, O earth and sea, for the devil has come down to you in fierce anger (fury), because he knows that he has [only] a short time [left]!

Revelation 12:12

147

Be Decisive!

Indecision wastes a lot of time, and time is too precious to waste. Become a decisive person, and you will accomplish a lot more with less effort.

No one learns to hear from God without making mistakes. Don't be overly concerned about errors. Don't take yourself too seriously. You are a fallible human being, not an infallible

god. Learn from your mistakes, correct the ones you can and continue being decisive.

If you believe it is right, then do it. That is how you will find out for sure. Devote a reasonable amount of time to waiting on God. Don't follow fleshly zeal, but do follow your heart.

Don't be afraid of yourself! You will not be the first person to make a mistake, nor will you be the last.

The fear of failure keeps thousands trapped in indecision, which definitely steals joy and complicates life.

Don't be afraid to make a decision and then follow through on it.

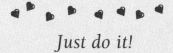

Just do it!

Did You Know?

*W*hen you try to gain freedom in your life, a spirit of fear will attempt to hold you in bondage. When God's day comes for you to be free, it's time to face the person or the situation that you are afraid of. It's time for you to walk up to people and talk to them, even if you are afraid. It's time to begin believing differently about yourself.

Fear will try to keep you in bondage. The only way you can get on the other side of it is to dig both heels in, set your face like a flint and say, "I know I've heard from God, and I'm going forward!"

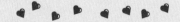

Remember: we live by faith, not by feelings.

Fruitfulness and Christian Witness

Rotten fruit comes
from rotten roots;
good fruit comes
from good roots.

Looking diligently lest any man fail of the grace of God; lest any root of bitterness springing up trouble you, and thereby many be defiled.

Hebrews 12:15 KJV

Our Witness

♥ ♥ ♥

I remember once when my entire family was in a restaurant eating, and the waitress tripped and dumped an entire tray of water, coffee and tea onto my husband. He was so kind and patient with her. He even talked with the manager to make sure the waitress did not get in any trouble. She had only been working there two weeks, and she was crying.

I am sure each of us can sense how she felt. She returned later with another tray of drinks, and as she leaned across the table to where I was sitting, she said, "I think I'm nervous because you're in here. I watch you on television all the time."

My heart rose up within me, "Oh, thank You, God. Thank You, thank You, thank You, that we did not act badly in this test."

We must realize how hurt others can be by our impatient behavior, and how it can adversely affect our witness.

By our fruits — our actions —
we shall be known.

153

Letting your light shine can be as simple as putting a smile on your face. That is one way to "flip on the switch" of God's glory.

Let your light so shine before men that they may see your moral excellence and your praiseworthy, noble, and good deeds and recognize and honor and praise and glorify your Father Who is in heaven.

Matthew 5:16

About the Author

Joyce Meyer has been teaching the Word of God since 1976 and in full-time ministry since 1980. As an associate pastor at Life Christian Center in St. Louis, Missouri, she developed, coordinated and taught a weekly meeting known as "Life In The Word." After more than five years, the Lord brought it to a conclusion, directing her to establish her own ministry and call it "Life In The Word, Inc."

Joyce's "Life In The Word" radio and television programs are heard or seen throughout the United States and the world. Her teaching tapes are enjoyed internationally. She travels extensively conducting Life In The Word conferences.

Joyce and her husband, Dave, business administrator at Life In The Word, have been married for over 34 years and are the parents of four children. All four children are married, and along with their spouses, work with Dave and Joyce in the ministry. Joyce and Dave reside in St. Louis, Missouri.

Joyce believes the call on her life is to establish believers in God's Word. She says, "Jesus died to set the captives free, and far too many Christians have little or no victory in their daily lives." Finding herself in the same situation many years ago, and having found freedom to live in victory through applying God's Word, Joyce goes equipped to set captives free and to exchange *ashes for beauty*. Joyce believes that every person who walks in victory leads many others into victory.

Joyce's life is transparent, and her teachings are practical and can be applied in everyday life.

Joyce has taught on emotional healing and related subjects in meetings all over the country, helping multiplied thousands. She has recorded more than 200 different audiocassette albums and is the author of 39 books to help the body of Christ on various topics.

Her "Emotional Healing Package" contains over 23 hours of teaching on the subject. Albums included in this package are: "Confidence"; "Beauty for Ashes" (includes a syllabus); "Managing Your Emotions"; "Bitterness, Resentment, and Unforgiveness"; "Root of Rejection"; and a 90-minute Scripture/music tape entitled "Healing the Brokenhearted."

Joyce's "Mind Package" features five different audio tape series on the subject of the mind. They include: "Mental Strongholds and Mindsets"; "Wilderness Mentality"; "The Mind of the Flesh"; "The Wandering, Wondering Mind"; and "Mind, Mouth, Moods, and Attitudes." The package also contains Joyce's powerful book, *Battlefield of the Mind*. On the subject of love she has three tape series entitled, "Love Is . . . "; "Love: The Ultimate Power"; and "Loving God, Loving Yourself, and Loving Others," and a book entitled, *Reduce Me to Love*.

Write to Joyce Meyer's office for a resource catalog and further information on how to obtain the tapes you need to bring total healing to your life.

To contact the author, write:

Joyce Meyer Ministries · P. O. Box 655 Fenton, Missouri 63026
or call: (636) 349-0303

Internet Address: www.joycemeyer.org

Please include your testimony or help received from this book when you write.
Your prayer requests are welcome.

To contact the author in Canada, please write:
Joyce Meyer Ministries Canada, Inc.
Lambeth Box 1300 · London, ON N6P 1T5
or call: (636) 349-0303

In Australia, please write:
Joyce Meyer Ministries-Australia
Locked Bag 77 · Mansfield Delivery Centre · Queensland 4122
or call: (07) 3349 1200

In England, please write:
Joyce Meyer Ministries · P. O. Box 1549 · Windsor SL4 1GT
or call: 01753 831102

Books by Joyce Meyer

The Harrison House Vision

Proclaiming the truth and the power
Of the Gospel of Jesus Christ
With excellence;

Challenging Christians to
Live victoriously,
Grow spiritually,
Know God intimately.